Living out loud on Facebook

Joanne Mazzotta

All opinions written in this book are those of the author.

      Joanne Mazzotta

This book is dedicated to all of the loves of my life…

"In our culture we are raised to think of ourselves as apart from community, apart from nature, apart from animals, apart from society apart from each other. But the reality is that we are completely intertwined in ways we don't even begin to understand."

Chuck Collins

THE TRUTH ABOUT FACEBOOK

May all those who find great messages on Facebook be aware that some of them are not true. After a fashion you will be able to pick and choose what you believe. There is a site that will help you determine what is true and what is not true.

SNOPES.COM

Carry on!

This phenomenon called Facebook that has swept the ground-breaking age of communication allows us to reach out to the entire universe. As we receive information in our pockets, on our desk tops, and within the confines of our art studios, cars, jobs, and kitchens; this vehicle of revolving forum filled with information seems infinite.

The true definition of humanity is one click away. True is the entire spectrum, the actual pull of life itself speaking to us day to day in ways we would not otherwise know, changing us in ways we could not have expected.

Sharing every aspect of life, sometimes unwelcomed aspects, Facebook lets us accept or deny according to our own needs the accessibilities of information, skill, suffering, hope, God, prayer, sickness, healing, counsel and song. We have become reachable… not always comfortably but easily.

People have begun to take humanity down off the shelf and express it on Facebook in ways that give others a peek behind their masks... It's clear to see how alike most of us are.
Joanne Mazzotta

While I am trying to find the words to describe what Facebook is, and how it affects our lives as if I were explaining it to a person born before Facebook became household word, I find it very difficult to explain … The very idea of it is so multifaceted due to the fact that Facebook is humankind.

Since I became a part of the Facebook community along with billions of others who in reality live on connected paths to the rest of the world I am changed because I am more aware of my authenticity. One of the most difficult things to do on Facebook i.e. the world is to be authentic because the urge to show only our best side looms large.

Those who do not engage in Facebook communications daily are parts of the minority. However, Facebook is not for everyone…

LURKERS

Of course there are millions of people who do not take part in Facebook.

There are however, the "lurkers" who read posts and do not react in any way. I believe there is a curiosity in all people. I don't feel spied on because I am consciously aware of myself and never post what I don't want others to see. But there are some who don't want to *be* seen so they will not reply or click the like button or even a smiley face because they will be seen. Facebook tells you who they are.

Clicking the LIKE button in reaction to a post on your newsfeed may be misinterpreted. We humans might have emotional reactions to such despite the fact that we are not speaking face to face.

Knowing what I post will remain in cyber space forever, I do not want my grandchildren to research my name when I'm looking down from the clouds and see anything disturbing. Negativity rests where I want it to rest.

I'm an idealist in every way. My words will not damage anyone I love. My upsetting thoughts don't appear in writing. Though I have my days, my basic stand is to live harmlessly.

I've seen what dark feelings and words can do to lives and sometimes I follow the lives of people who are constantly angry. I never fail to find them falling into one of the bad energy wagons… Yes, every action gets an equal and opposite reaction and their good fortune is out of the range of peaceful living.

The laws of attraction are valid and when someone, anyone reeks of hate and anger it invites thousands of replies of the same nature. The stench of hateful replies goes on for days as the infection spreads.

LOVE, LOVE, LOVE... SERIOUSLY?

Some have doubted that many replies to posts contain true love when they see loving reactions to beautiful images, stories of survival and encouraging words. Of course it may be true that those love gurus may not live the way they claim. In fact some are living in the mire of wretchedness but sweet as sugar in some replies on Facebook. They're easy to catch. When Facebook members claim love and a day later spout hatred for their neighbor in a post, they're caught!

I've seen references of love in thousands of reports on Facebook in thousands of ways. As if love were something to unpack it would have enormous weight and it hits my heart and continues to do so daily. Almost every time I read posts filled with truth, I find it... I found delight in videos of children dancing, singing, and playing with puppies and in songs.

Love shows up in art, passion for helping the hungry, quotes by great authors about God in all his glory and in historic moments, respect for our veterans of every war, and in simple words from one mind to another. Love is all that matters when you cut through the exposure of broken hearts.

As Dante wrote in the ending of The Divine Comedy, *"It is love that moves the sun and other stars."*

THE FUTURE

Facebook babies come into this world on social media starting from sonogram photos to their first birthdays then on to proms, college graduations to their weddings and I have enjoyed them as I watched them grow up. Watching their lives unfold adds pleasure to my days. It is apparent to me that these children will grow up in a very different world than I did. If one day we meet one of those babies we can say, "I met you before you were born… *on* Facebook."

I wonder if social media will be a part of who they become and I am concerned that one day they won't have relationships face to face, touch to touch, and heart to heart. Nonetheless, I've enjoyed them growing from babies to young adults making parents proud by doing things that I would have never been exposed to if not for Facebook. Children today are brilliant at ages baby boomers were never challenged to become.

Technology is no stranger to a toddler now days.

I am guilty of sharing the lives of my own children *on* Facebook for no other reason than to show them off... No matter how beautiful and no matter that I see them as God's works of art, I know what photos not to post. Those who know me as a Facebook friend also know my children give the words pride and joy new meanings to me.

I've made wonderful friends with people all over the world I would never have known if not for Facebook and have invited them to my country and my table.

THE DISTORTION OF SOCIAL MEDIA

To make someone who is not sensitive to what Facebook is and does not understand it would take many books.

I am prepared for attack but I will say it anyway. Facebook is one of the tools God uses today to bring about love from every corner of the world. Facebook is his vehicle! It brings us to the new lives that enter the earth and to the transitions of angels from earth to heaven. It brings us to the bed sides of many people who are dying; those we have come to love and those whose lives have blessed our own.

Facebook allows us the privilege of knowing and caring for entire families who live on the other side of the world.

We trim our lives via Facebook and we can send good energy into the universe with this tool of God's. We are instruments of this journey we were given, no matter how painful, no matter how blissful.

This morning while my heart felt like it would break for my dearest 39 year old nephew who is in the mire of a disease we all dread and fear, Cancer. He is facing the light that is so near, his face is glowing. He smiles and tells us not to worry. He is at peace with it. That makes me cry more because he won the trial of love for us with flying colors. Robert could love like no other. His fate devastated hundreds. Almost to the minute I began to question God, my beloved grandchildren showed up in living color in a video on my Facebook newsfeed page and took me back to hope and faith. As children they know no dread, anxiety or dismay. They were dancing while Robbie was preparing to go home.

Facebook validates our feelings in so many ways. I have found delightful moments on this universal round-table during the worst of times.

Poignant moments can arrive in the middle of the night when we open our Facebook link and read posts written by other insomniacs who choose to get lost in a unique experience instead of arguing with sleep.

I met Dalai Lama on Facebook at 2:00 AM.

He was just sitting there

Waiting for me to notice him.

One of the best parts of Facebook is, it is a place where we can remove toxic energy from our life circle with one click.

Joanne Mazzotta

TO BE ONE

More than once while reading posts on Facebook I was able to identify with the writer. I felt less alone in my feelings that matched the writer's feelings. Unlike real life engaging I am able to get a clear message when someone speaks in the written word. I've often tapped into inspirational sites that appear almost immediately after a Facebook friend speaks to sadness, loneliness and repeated displays of sorrow. I began to wonder if the entire Facebook community suffered from depression. I know now that is not true. Rather, people tell tales of sorrow because sorrow is a part of who we are. No one is exempt from sadness.

THE WORLD AND LIFE ON MANY LEVELS

Tonight while feeling restless and unable to sleep I sat before my laptop, opened my Facebook link and enjoyed seeing a five year old girl singing Frank Sinatra's rendition of, Fly Me to The Moon. It was almost a Zen moment. I watched that video many times and it was better than any ad asking me to buy a book about anxiety or depression. It did more than any Buddha could for my cluttered mind that often insists that I worry about things that will never happen.

Speaking of ads, hundreds and thousands of ads appear on Facebook. I believe it is the most amazing marketing tool in the world. When you open a link about any item you can think of, ads for similar products will begin to appear on your Facebook wall. Many of them can lure sales. I believe irrefutably that it affects our economy in ways nothing else can.

BITS AND PIECES OF LIFE

Photos of events and videos of living people in the acts of humanity flood Facebook from minute to minute. Some have restored my faith and some have caused me to learn what is and is not real. The great tease happens when the post has guilt between the lines while telling you to reply and share if you care. It hasn't been proven that those kinds of posters have an agenda.

Some posts make me cry tears of joy like when I watch a baby being born or read a story of survival. The endurance of human beings after a tragedy can build more strength in me than I realized I owned.

My compassion rises when I read a story with photos posted by a parent of a struggling child with a terminal disease who smiles while lying in a hospital bed as nurses sing to him or when I see a mother standing at a podium speaking to sorrow with the courage of an angel whose wings have been scorched.

Almost one hundred percent of parents will share moments with their children on Facebook. Beautiful children dot the pages while posing for the camera. It's clear that children born on Facebook know how to pose as well as any professional model. When children see a camera they are stopped in their tracks and at once put on their amusement faces. The smiles are instantaneous. The best ones are the
Videos that go viral often show babies laughing. The sound of the famous quintuplets laughing hysterically while in bed with their momma gets into my head like an ear worm. I'm sure those babies are in school now but Facebook shows them again and again, year after year like a jewel we take out to admire on occasion, a jewel that sounds like angel bells.

MAKING FRIENDS

Discussions are born when we see pictures of the lives of people we never met, their puppies, kittens, cars, homes, gardens, and an array of moments they spend traveling. . Often they turn into friendships and those friendships become genuine relationships that last for years. I've met many people on Facebook this applies to.

I attended an art class that I learned about *on* Facebook. When I walked into the class, the art instructor whom I never met in person knew my name because of my Facebook profile picture. We "friended" each other on Facebook later and I was blessed to see his paintings, eat at his restaurants and simply put, his life added something to my life because of Facebook.

Using the term, "*On* Facebook" doesn't sound strange anymore. As if Facebook was a rock or a hill, a TV, raft, boat, horse, 'the dock of the bay' or time itself, we use the term like it has always been part of our language.

Because my adult children are, '*on*' Facebook I get to enjoy their posts and photos of my grandchildren, some old enough to be able to post as well. I am able to visit my nieces and nephews who live out of state and share moments of their lives better than (what is now called) 'snail mail' could possibly help me do. We have made plans together on Facebook in a snap which brought us to airports and gatherings in each other's homes. Facebook has become a household word because it's become an accepted a way to connect.

One sleepless night while my beloved nephew was laying in wait for the light in a hospice facility in Florida, I received a text message from my other nephew at 1:00 AM. He said, "Please come auntie, my mother (my sister) needs you." Within minutes I got a ticket from RI to Florida. I was there at 6:00PM. *Because of Facebook!*

TO LIKE OR NOT TO LIKE

One of the features on Facebook is the ***LIKE*** button with a picture of thumbs up... How free we are to be given permission to like a person, a picture or a post. We can literally compliment the thoughts of others. The choice to respond to thoughts by clicking - LIKE-LAUGH-CRY-ANGRY icons or scroll past quickly is a freedom. I've seen some words I'd rather not let into my psych and some that compel me to respond.

While overhearing a conversation while at the supermarket I had to chuckle. A woman embraced another woman she ran into there and after exchanging greetings, one of them asked, "Hey, why did you unfriend me on Facebook?" The other replied, "Because you never click ***LIKE*** on any of my posts."

I'm careful not to post downbeat ideas thereby fanning the flames of those literary pieces that may invite insult in any way. As a friend of mine once said, "Facebook is for polite chit chat." Perhaps that was what was originally intended by the makers of Facebook but it has gone very far beyond that.

HELL ON FACEBOOK

I saw a video shot in Boston the night of the terrorist attack by two brothers. They were seen on camera carrying a bomb that killed people watching the Boston Marathon while standing on the sidewalk. The injuries were clear and the terror was obvious. And we saw this on Facebook. These stories accompanied by photos and videos are not fiction. Nonfiction couldn't be as bad.

POLITICS

Political postings on Facebook in great quantities during the 2016 presidential campaign has afforded me the ability to appreciate that not everything we face can be changed but nothing can be changed until it is faced.

I had not known Albert Einstein said, *"If I were to remain silent, I'd be guilty of complicity."* And I do believe he said it.

Social Media often causes (some) people react like the *Pied Piper* or the mice that followed him.

And it makes people believe things that yell out to the triggers of their inner core.... In other words they believe everything they read, especially if it is negative which I believe taps into their own personal anger issues and gives their deepest rage a hook to hang them on.

I have no opinion of Donald Trump. He doesn't live with me. Perhaps if he visited me, cut my grass, walked my dog, broke bread with my big

Italian family I'd have an opinion of him. And yet I've come to understand that Facebook is a doorway where all emotions can enter, and "hate" is ready to express itself in the large, worldly community called "Social Media" whereby it becomes contagious like a septic flu and can overtake the entire forum creating a mass amount of influence to the actual powers that be. If you think those powers don't read Facebook, think again.

Facebook can become a fertile setting for loss of verbal caution. It can cause people to agree with the haters and pass forward extreme dislike and destruction to the world without realizing we've been influenced by the hypothesis of some stranger. The bad news is, each hateful post fully defines the millions of glass houses we live in when we throw verbal stones. The good news is, Facebook members can choose wisely what they read.

WHAT IS MEDIA?

Has anyone wondered if Facebook has replaced TV?

TV keeps us informed of the location of a hurricane but Facebook does it better and faster. More than this we can see the personal effects of storms that ravish lives. Not always pleasant, those times and people get into our psych's and inspire us to do two things, be grateful and pray. Usually what is accompanied by destruction is humanity at its best.

Some spend more time on Facebook than they do watching TV.

TRAVELING SHOW

My good friends Carla and Michael are not celebrities according to the world but are celebrities on Facebook which is the world by way of two billion people. They are both currently in Paris.

I saw in living color what they ate for breakfast and they took us all along with them to Italy last week teasing us with the food and scenery. It's not a National Geographic page of pictures taken by strangers and altered to perfect specifications. It is real life friends sharing their travels with us and others who check Facebook while enjoying their first morning coffee. I like that about Facebook.

I like Italy.

Now I like Paris too.

THANK YOU FACEBOOK

Some ask, (though few) "What is Facebook?
What can be bad about it?
The bad is the lightly poisoned delight some get out of vile reports on life and its doings. If the adage, "Like attracts like" is true, it was never more pronounced. Facebook has made it so in the way some need to express their negative ideas publicly and gather others to agree with them. To what purpose or gain can a billion followers offer? I'm not sure but to achieve celebrity status on Facebook is no minor thing now days. A Facebook membership can offer more than ego satisfaction, it can make you money. Yes, Facebook is a very popular way to market your wares. The ads that pop up while you open a link can be annoying for sure but buying products made available through those ads are already popular to the point where small businesses are closing because we can shop from our chairs. Guilty!

As photographs of children and family members abound on Facebook no one can attack a member for posting selfies. By the way that word, "Selfies" is not yet in our dictionary but I'm sure it will be soon. Everyone without exception (but for the lurkers) post selfies or some form of photos of themselves.

Most selfies are beautiful and some are photo shopped. We want to look our best. To share your "self" with the world is a generous act. I believe it helps us relate to others in ways we were unable to in the past.

The words, ("How ya doing?") are no longer necessary. We know how everyone is doing and all we have to do is turn on our devices to check in with people we call friends and family. In fact if we don't see those people posting or responding for a while, we contact them to be sure they're doing well. If not we wish them well.

When anyone posts about their flu, broken leg, surgery etc. we see hundreds of replies like this;

"Get well soon.

I hope you feel better.

I'm sorry you're sick.

Try ___, it helped me.

Oh no! Please feel better!"

TV- CELL PHONES- AND FACEBOOK

While watching a movie recently I saw cell phones dramatically involved in character parts. I've also heard actors refer to "Facebook" in their scripted dialog in several movies. I guess Facebook is now a real part of life in every arena.

At first I was surprised.

I'm no longer surprised.

Does Facebook prevent Alzheimer's disease? Older people who live and spend many hours alone get their brains stimulated by Facebook because there are many people to talk to that inspire their minds to consider more than four walls.

So that would be a yes.

A GRIEF GURU'S WARM WELCOME TO THE TUNNEL

I describe grief as a tunnel because that is where I healed. It is dark in there. No light shines until time lights up the avenue crowded with others in the tunnel you haven't noticed. It is that moment those hurting souls see they are not alone nor are they crazy.

To be a part of something greater than your own pain is the path to healing. Facebook allows us to meet others in that tunnel. We speak to death, to heartache, to life, and to love and we embrace (*On Facebook.*)

SORROW

It's November. Not my favorite time of year... As it goes; "*There is strength in numbers*" and the decision to live life after the death of a special loved one is most important. We must live it in joy and peace or not live it at all as we lift each other in November. We begin to live ten minutes at a time while our lives become split into the *before and after* a tragedy.

You can't know grief until it hits you like an amputation of your emotional legs leaving you to crawl back to yourself, back to your life; a life you are no longer a part of yet there is a population of millions of others who are barely peripheral as you heal with eyes that cannot see forward. You will meet others that know grief in ways that rock your soul. The piece of you that fell off is replaced with a piece of you only grief can create. Compassion, empathy and the true meaning of love walks with you forever and drags you out of life's margins.

Facebook is a place to turn because sleep doesn't come with tears. It's always there no matter what time of day or night. I've used it myself to talk to others in grief and to share my darkest moments until one of them writes the words I need to hear in the form of *Ted Talks* or they might stir me with beautiful videos that speak to life and death. Above is a recent Facebook post I wrote to express and help people who even for an instant believe they are alone in their pain after losing a loved one. In addition to the book I wrote after my 32 year old son Danny died titled, WHY WHISPER? takes the reader to my world after his suicide I stay sensitive to the grief journey that remains widespread no matter what loved one dies. Yes, it is said that losing a child is the worst kind of grief possible. I agree... My book speaks to the myriad of ways grief changes us, where it puts us, and what the first reactions look like. If you read my book, Why Whisper? You've read my heart after my son left earth and you've read your own.

Those who have had to bury a child visit the place where all parents go when their child is gone between the lines of written grief that has no definition. I've not yet read or have been able to draw a parallel to the feeling. Even Elizabeth Kubler Ross was unable to define this brand of pain in her famous *Five Stages*. In comparison to her stages grief over the loss of a child is like falling down an endless flight of stairs, flailing and never landing long enough to inspect the injuries and not caring to.

Crazy takes on a new meaning, with a new addition to itself. That addition brings you to understand others who have suffered loss. It doesn't happen suddenly but we begin to appreciate those who understand why nothing in life should be taken for granted and yet we begin to make a choice to live on with our new perspective and to accept we are fallible and vulnerable every day we live.

Broken hearts don't always heal, sometimes they just stop beating. The option to go on or not go on is persistent for the rest of our lives. To die while we live is easier than to choose to go on searching for relief ... And yet, you might *want* to experience newborn babies smiling, love from good friends, wonderful people achieving their dreams, sunsets that only God can paint, the joy of seeing others make it through the hardest of times, and you want to be one of them. There are definitely times when someone appears on Facebook the moment you need them to walk you off the ledge.

Do we adapt? Yes. And we can do it by exchanging thoughts with others on a platform we crawl on until we find our new legs.

LIVING AND DYING ON FACEBOOK

Millions of Facebook members woke up to a devastating post about a beloved Facebook friend who learned that her beautiful son died and she shared his obituary with the world.

Immediately replies rushed in to embrace her with loving words.

Unlike traditional wakes when people hug you and say they're sorry for your loss then go home to leave you alone with your pain, Facebook keeps you embraced for as long as you need some healing. It gives your grief a right to be heard and attracts others who lead you to the places where you find those who understand.

Jessica Mastascusa Streaty

January 29, 2017 ·

My Niece shared my nephews last moments on Facebook...and brought thousands of kind hearts to his bedside.

"Rob's last days.... into the very final and ever so beautiful moment that he gifted us with. Days before the 26th, I spoke to Rob about calling upon God. I mentioned how HE had to call him... and that he would feel true peace.

Rob immediately asked me what he should call God. I told him he could call him whatever he wanted.... but that he needed to make contact!

Rob then asked me if he could call him Scott, like "our Scott Read"... I assured him that God would answer to that name too! On the day of his transition, I had gone back to his house to tidy up some. While in the front closet, my aunt had picked up a bag and out of this dropped random photo from 2004 of Scott dressed as Santa with Rob. My heart melted.

When I returned to Hospice, Robert Mastascusa's eyes were wide open! (For the first time in weeks!) I immediately showed him the photo and reminisced of the days of Santa and Scott... Rob then gave the most beautiful smile and one little tear drop glistened as it dripped down his cheek. I then walked around to the opposite side of the bed to show Mommy how to read texts on her new phone. I read out-loud the very last text I sent her.

"Hi Mom! Please read this out loud to Robbie. Let him know that the utilities have been turned on in your condo unit. You are ALL set! Thanks Blue!"

It was at THAT VERY MOMENT when Rob took his last deep breath, so beautiful, so peaceful...

Mom and I then walked around the bed, mommy asked Blue (Rob) if it was Daddy who she heard calling her name when she was napping moments earlier. Rob then let out one last quiet sound accompanied by the most magical smile ever...

And it was at that moment Rob made the transition home to our maker!

I am ABSOLUTELY CERTAIN that Robbie is safe now and FOREVER with us!!!

I love you Blue!! I love you with all that I am from deepest depth of my soul! Thank you my brother for being beautiful beyond reason!!! Thank you for taking care of us all!"

We LOVE YOU for being YOU!!!
Miles of smiles and gracious gratitude!

A sister's love, devotion and tender truth carried out in a way I have never seen in my life and probably never will again. She helped him go home with dignity.

THE SORROW RACE

Don't try to win a race with grief. It will beat you and meet you at the finish line. And the finish line keeps moving. Walk with it so you don't run out of breath. Grief needs a right to be heard and a home in your heart of hearts where it becomes a part of who you are.

Until we meet again my precious angels...

TOUCH AND BONDS

If someone asked me how Facebook has changed my life, the first thing I would say is, "My Facebook writer friend who lives in Australia, traveled all that way to visit me in Rhode Island for a few days. She and her son ate at my table, slept in my guest room and enjoyed her stay in my home. My husband and I enjoyed them. I felt a sisterly bond with her while listening to her incredible life story. She once entertained the troupes in Vietnam. She lived in many different parts of the world and adopted six hungry, homeless children in her travels. Because June Collins broke bread with me I am wiser for it. If not for Facebook I would have never met her, read her books or shared many hours chatting about our lives face to face.

Her book, **'Goodbye Junie Moon'** takes readers to her life in Vietnam when women didn't travel to such places.

I read this intense saga wondering how this story will end. The author, June Collins puts you in a posture that keeps you reading without distraction. Her nonfiction story takes you to a place where most Americans dared not go.

June Collins takes you with her to places in the world most people in the western world do not know about, or think of. She brings you to the inequalities, the prejudices, and the injustices in countries in Asia, from Manila, Hong Kong, Bangkok, Taipei, Singapore, Kuala Lumpur, Korea, Japan and Vietnam; while she gently allows you follow her through her embryonic conditionings as an Australian native. Her childhood sorrows and young adult shocks draw the outline for the buildup of her stunning portrait that could have cost her life.

Collin's writing gives a clear vision (to the reader) - of the Vietnam War in plain English from the prospective of a woman who seemed to have no fear. A flow keeps you reading while she seems to be speaking directly to the situations she found herself in or rather, where she finds (herself.) Born to a mother who was every bit a lady with staunch moral codes and home based values it seems unlikely that she could have turned some of the incredible corners she did which lays to rest the old myth that there exists a nature verses nurture promise. The rendition of her childhood could not have dictated her life as a traveling exotic dancer. Her story would cause Freud to put his notes into the fire.

Several books I've read this year took me to Vietnam, but this one takes me there as a woman. Her initial introduction to a war torn country in the 1960's was horribly frightening, but she tells of it as if it were a stormy day in a park. She was a woman alone in Vietnam during a devastating war, to entertain troops. At first I couldn't make up my mind if June was courageous, audacious or just plain crazy. I saw no fear between the lines of her book but rather extraordinary curiosity and courage. It was as if her guts crossed paths with her good sense while she exchanged her sarcasm with her conduit, O 'Halloran - the man who brought her there unaware she would not allow him to prostitute her many talents became the springboard to her fate in Vietnam.

From the read I learned how deadly honesty could conceivably be. I speak for myself as one who has not traveled to places this author brought me to until I read this astonishing story. Nothing in June Collins' book is predictable when she finds herself in Vietnam for three and a half years as an entertainer... While the horrors of that war, the underhanded politics and the extreme experiences there saddened me deeply but not as deeply as when she placed violets on her dead baby's grave. I'm not sure which impression moved me the most, her story or that woman who survived her story! The most profound quote in June Collin's narrative is, "Like the old saying goes, *"You've never really lived until you've nearly died."*

Another one of my many incredible friendships developed with a Florida woman who was introduced to me via a local Rhode Island friend who met her in Italy while traveling. After we connected on Facebook I now call her my friend and sister. Terry Oxtal and her husband Doug lost a son as I did. That brought them to a new dimension they were not prepared for.

My new Floridian Facebook friend told me about the journals she kept after losing her son Andrew to a hospital mistake and when I told her to publish them she asked if I would read them which I did. Together we created a book called, **Life After the Death of My Child**, now available on Amazonbooks.com. How could I have experienced that if not for Facebook?

Sometimes the definition of "FRIEND" is genuine.

I have met and housed Facebook friends from Norway, Europe, California, Australia, and Florida.

Before meeting them in person it was clear to me who they were, how they thought and almost how their hearts beat. Facebook offers up a picture that cannot be seen with the eyes. After the friendship developed we remained in touch and shared parts of our lives on a regular basis like good friends do.

LAUGHING OUT LOUD

There is hardly a morning, as I sit at my perch with my coffee that I don't see something on Facebook that makes me laugh.

This morning I saw a video of a 3 year old child dancing to the Jailhouse Rock

How else but for Facebook could I have known those people?

The Facebook voyage can take you from photos of gorgeous flowers to a fund raiser for a child with cancer within minutes. It sounds illogical and yet it is an internet reality.

My mind is frequently challenged to think *out of the box*, if you will. In fact, there is no box, only a vast spectrum of life in every inch of a forum that has in its hands a sort of entity. Whether it is a debate or a shared quote by Albert Einstein, there is never a time when realizations don't surprise me while reading Facebook.

Can an Atheist meet God on Facebook?

Probably …

EMOTION VIA SOCIAL MEDIA

As a mouthpiece for those who are lonely or estranged from family Facebook offers a doorway to exchange sentiment, however twisted or subdued. These emotions can vary from how hard life is, how sick one is and how hateful or loving one can be. Those posts interest me. They also teach by silent observation that however many people have hurt me, I have bitten back... What a lesson! At the same time we watch other posters console, give advice and send out many cyber hugs to no end while the angry one stays angry and will soon return with prattles of hatful words about the bad hand life has dealt them consistently. I've not tried to save them; they apparently like it that way.

There is a huge amount of misbehavior and subtle hints meant for a person no one knows and no one will get the message but that one person. It didn't take me long to roll past those posts. They are not meant for me. But I still smile when adult children misbehave.

HIDING ON FACEBOOK

All humans have sins and secrets. Some find it relieving to share those on Facebook with total strangers which may lead to judgments of no real worth. If not their own sins and secrets many share those of others… like celebrities. It can get like a gossip column on steroids. I'm not sure how that helps them to align themselves with the right side of the street. I'm not qualified to evaluate that kind of behavior but am also not one to take part in it. It doesn't help anything. It doesn't make me feel better.

I grew up in the 60's in a world filled with those who found some kind of pleasure in scandal. To this day I won't indulge in it. It is fact that when more than one person knows something it is not a secret. What I learned at my childhood kitchen table cost me many hours sitting opposite a qualified expert who eventually convinced me I was worthy of love. (*That's one of my secrets.*)

Another few secrets are, I'm deaf on my left side. When a soft spoken person speaks to me, I listen with my eyes.

I am probably mildly dyslexic. No one knows how hard it is for me to express myself in writing when I'm working on a book. It often takes me too long to compose a sentence while moving words and letters around. I have to look away from a paragraph for a day only to come back to it with a different point of examination.

Before I publish anything I've written I may have to edit it many times to make the message clear. Some words might be written backwards. Punctuation offers the same problems. I read my words out loud when I think I've completed editing a manuscript multiple times and always there are more grammatical errors.

The only way I can trust my work is if my husband reads it out loud and much to my surprise he finds errors I didn't notice when I would have bet the farm there were none.

What we expose on Facebook varies from person to person. Some post photographs of their injuries, successes and their failures. Those injuries might be the kinds that live within the posters heart. We see divorces, attacks on parents, government, doctors or neighbors, and sadly, attacks on other posters. Facebook makes us laugh and makes us shed tears. What we see we react to of course if we chose to read through long posts describing emotions felt by the writer. Those are the posts I like to read because it is an ongoing novel, some fact, some fiction but written with care. If someone takes the time to share their pain, joy, fear, shock and love, I have the time to read it and respond kindly.

ANGER CAN HEMORRAGE

What we see with our eyes goes into our souls. I vigilantly scroll past words that contain hatred. With the touch of a button we can save ourselves the infection of someone's loathing.

There is no fear of being stalked on Facebook. We are able to block any person and the posts they write are no longer visible to us.

MUSIC and LOVE

In the midst of a summer morning ads for waterproof mascara alongside news of the death of a celebrity, Facebook's way of causing your mind to move fast is never ending. The effortless joy of a three year old singing and dancing or a birthday party offering children and adults making fun of themselves can bring a smile to your face. But music compels me to stop thinking and enter the realm of peace, memories and escape. Facebook members post music of all kinds and I always thank them when a song hits my heart softly while I struggle to find sleep. Some music is pure prayer.

LINKS TO FAR AWAY PLACES

As we travel through our Facebook moments it is not absurd to imagine traveling throughout history to hear "*dead poets*" speak to life as it was then but I notice emotions then were not very different from life now. Poems by Lord Byron and quotes by Shakespeare speak out loudly to the same kind of love, heartaches and fears. Thousands of years have not changed the human condition.

Some believe the world has gotten worse. I don't. I believe rather that life is now on a wider stage and social media has brought it all to our tables.

Rape, murder, failures and triumphs are no more integrated to our existence than they were in the 1800's; we simply get the news faster.

Remember Jack the Ripper, Son of Sam, Charles Manson, Adolf Hitler, and of course the murder of Jesus Christ by Pontius Pilate who called for his death. The people killed him, the judgments and the mob mentality concept killed him. Are we afraid if we allow our kindness and love to come to the surface they will kill us like they killed Jesus? We see this fact on Facebook every day when posters say they love you and they don't and when they give you a *like* when they don't like. I see that behavior as a cry for love.

There is that sector of posters who need love so badly they will reach out for it in various ways. And there are the lonely who want to bring you to their houses and remain a recluse at the same time. They must feel safe interacting with a guarantee that no one will point out their inability to socialize in person. No one will call you out.

I see some Facebook members show off their worth, as if you are only worth what you have. To me, that is the central lie and the biggest myth in life.

Most of us enjoy those pictures. Some would rather see the poster share their shame, poverty, and problems, then get annoyed because they think the owners of good fortune are lying or at the very least showing off. It's a mixed bag of human frailties spread out on a table made of effective, virtual reality in photographs.

WHO CARES?

Food is a draw on Facebook. One may be surprised who cares about what you cooked. I once posted a photo of over a hundred cooked meatballs I made for a very special occasion. It tickled me to see the multiple likes and comments I received on my picture posts. In fact tonight I cooked a meal because of a recipe shared on Facebook by a friend.

When I see scrumptious meals and the videos that show how it is cooked, I get happy. I'm not always happy to see sweet desserts in the middle of the night, however.

Smiley faces are plentiful when anyone posts their restaurant meals. I'm guessing the Facebook family is a bunch of foodies. Due to my own ethnic genes, I see food as a celebration.

Who cares that you have the flu? Who cares that a tree fell on your property during a hurricane and who cares what you look like in your new shoes?

Who cares what you looked like 30 years ago, or how your children look today? Who cares that your lawn is greener this year or that your flowers bloomed in spring? Who cares if your husband had a heart attack or what you wore to the prom? People do care.

Every talent bares a share. Writers, artists, singers, and the amazing creations done by gifted people all over the world are gifts to us while we stroll along Facebook...

Of course there are posts that go "Viral" and reach people all over the earth.

Of course I have pain and dark days, but who cares? And if people do care as some of my real life friends do, how does that kill off the dark dog that rears its head in my life? What it does do is make me recognize other people's pain and that's when my empathy becomes immediate.

The original definition of compassion is, *"to suffer with."*

Often Facebook has brought terminal illness of a Facebook friend or a loved one to our attention. We watch the process as daily reports of the sickness inflame our concern and we take them with us in our own daily lives as we would a family member.

While trying to understand who cares that you're doing laundry or eating spaghetti at 3:00 AM. I imagine it's easier to keep the *likes* flowing for those things than to feel someone else's pain though some identify more with depressing posts than they do with light hearted posts. We search for humor on sleepless nights but often find painful stories of broken lives.

RAISING MONEY ON FACEBOOK

For those who need it desperately…

I have witnessed the ability to raise money for those who have needed it for medical expenses, funerals, and other maladies that have attacked lives unexpectedly. This is real! Yes, I have donated money to many worthy causes I was made aware of on Facebook and thank God I could.

Go Fund Me is a link that becomes a way to help others financially to help pay for things like, a single father's inability to pay for medication for one of his five children with a terminal illness. I've seen thousands of dollars raised in minutes when a background story is posted about a car accident that killed a sister or brother whose family had no life insurance. I've also seen people give to the causes that afflict people in the name of medical care. Facebook offers a way to contribute to important causes every day and remain anonymous.

Lives have been saved because of Facebook. The amazing grace of people who care, strangers who contribute to others in need and the reality of goodness in people all over the world make me love better.

THE ART OF Facebook...

Tonight, while I couldn't sleep I opened my Facebook page to find an author and a painter I knew nothing about. I read biographies posted by two of my favorite Facebook friends that I never met in person yet have known for several years in my Facebook community. I enjoyed the information and the photos of these artists and learned things I would have never known if not for Facebook.

It occurred to me that Facebook is a kind of art of its own. With such a wide door into the lives of those posthumous and those alive today and to the magnificent way Facebook connects us all, I am grateful to enter cautiously with regard for how it can be misused. Once we pass through the threshold it is the actual world we enter, share, and speak to. There is no way we can ignore the joy and pain of other humans. What surrounds us in the Facebook world surrounds us in the virtual world.

I have enjoyed art on many levels because of Facebook. Some creations that were fashioned by the historians who died hungry and despite that, their works hang in museums today and are worth millions of dollars. Some creations were shared by living artists I now call friends. To my entertainment I surrender to the reflections of the minds on canvas displayed in ways no one may see if not for cell phones and home computers, which brings me to the magic of technology.

MEDICAL TREATMENT CELL PHONES

I was standing in the local Wound Center in my city while my husband was laying in a bed being treated for a leg wound. As I was admiring the nurse who worked on him and how she exemplified perfect skill when suddenly her cell phone that lay on the dressing table approximately four feet away made the familiar sound that beckons the owner to answer it. She immediately left my husband half way through the treatment she was giving him to walk quickly to her phone, press a button and picked it up staring at the screen. In this day and age I shouldn't be surprised to see that, but I was. In fact I was frightened.

I have witnessed employees buying shoes via the internet during work hours. It doesn't surprise me to see clerks in stores, wait staff in restaurants, doctors in examining rooms, drivers on the turnpike, and yes nurses in the middle of treating a patient take a time out to respond to a pinging cell phone on a table in a treatment room.

It leaves me to wonder why grandmothers have cell phones, and why toddlers have them in their hands while strapped into car seats.

It's true my peers have the world in their purses captured in a very small thin box that may jingle while they shop. I've seen many people with a cell phone clasped to their ears in supermarkets while talking loudly in the vegetable aisle. It almost embarrasses me when I can hear their conversations. I'm going to guess that one day we will become accustomed to stores filled with white noise.

I've seen the same behavior in church, at dinner tables, in school classrooms, restaurants, banks and even police and School bus drivers are scanning the road unconsciously while listening to information through cell phones stuck to their ears.

Car accidents caused by drivers who are not focused on the road in front of them have crashed into stopped vehicles and caused their own deaths because of a cell phone that is getting the attention the road should.

I read an article about walkers on crowded sidewalks in New York City who are getting and causing injuries due to cell phone use. Walkers! People with cell phones are in danger constantly. The recent report of deaths caused by cell phone use exceeds the former drunk driver death toll. Being a casualty of cell phone addiction may be worse than drugs. Actually it seems cell phones *are* a sort of drug. Try taking one away from a teen!

Technology is a gift to our world in many ways. It took genius to create it and it is sometimes hazy. If the biblical advice, *"Nothing in excess"* applies to technology it is a problem instead of a contribution to the social order. It has run ramped in society today along with email, texting, and phone calls. Thumbs and other fingers are moving faster every day. When I see people texting in vehicles, on bikes and while walking across streets, I am alarmed.

Have ways of communications these days lessened our ability to reach out in person? That possibility may give us a feeling of unease …

Most profile quotes appear on the left side of every poster's page. If you need to research the poster in order to decide whether to friend them or not you will get a gut feeling about that person and base your decision on their life quote.

My favorite…

Jessica Mastascusa Streaty's life quote

"Thank you GOD"

FACEBOOK FUNK

While it is hardly a mystery that people are not always aware of themselves when they speak with their keyboard voice, with a few exceptions.

Facebook is sharing *memories* every day which allows us to look back at the words and thoughts posted in the past and see clearly how we've changed through the years.

Facebook can be likened to magic carpet that slows down enough to allow you to board it. It safely allows you to feel virtual wind in your hair while it flies over the world. Your voice in response to cries for help, gentle prodding or the ability to share reactions to the valued moments shared by others can be felt on a universal level. Your magic carpet can fly over Italy and minutes later you can find yourself in Egypt by invite from a friend visiting there. You may see foods that tempt your appetite, or a colorful door in the heart of Greece in real time. Facebook has blown the doors off National Geographics. We no longer need that once famous magazine.

Minutes later you might see a video of someone's grandchild hitting a home run, and you have to smile. Facebook brings the soft ball field to you.

Posting parts of your life you are not ashamed to share can inspire others to respond. One night my sister, who lives 1500 miles away said to me, "I can see your whole life on Facebook." I laughed and said, "If I didn't want anyone to see it I wouldn't post it." Little did she know what I don't share. She is one of the people who are intimidated by social media... Options galore are the great thing about Facebook. How you use them is your choice and no one else's. Sure, some things we see on Facebook are not comfortable but as I said somewhere in this book, we have a delete button and should use it when we need to. The good, the bad and the ugly will always live loudly in humanity and Facebook is humanity.

To my pleasure I am able to use the privacy feature allowed on Facebook. I decide who can see what I post. Sometimes I am in a deep mood; A dark place where I feel the need to vent, and do. I reach out because I can, and the responses are always kind.

Anniversaries of a lost loved one are heavy. The many mothers who have had to experience the shock and pain of a child's death often soothe me and hold me in their cyber arms until the anniversary passes. And repeatedly, no matter how healed I think I am Facebook allows me to free my sorrow when it hits … without shame.

My favorite posts are always repeated stories and photos of children. I saw and heard a five year old child singing opera. I saw a four year old boy play Mozart on his piano. I giggled out loud when I saw a child tell his mother to "listen, listen Linda!"

I'm guilty of sharing moments with my eight grandchildren. I don't deny being proud and blessed to have them and to love them.

Facebook life can be felt through the typed word and hope can become barefaced.

I pray I have given hope to those who were stuck in a marsh of pain. I always want to help them recognize they are not in a hole but the hole is in them...

I love children because they are free. They live in the moment not the past or future. We were children once, where did that magnificent God like part of us go? Even Google cannot answer that question.

SEE YA ON FACEBOOK!

Parting words while in the embraces of my adult children with a kiss on the cheek at the end of a visit, the words, and "See ya on Facebook" is always followed by a giggle.

Yes, Facebook is occupied by parents and adult children daily. Often I will receive a word of love or a photo of my grandchildren while they play, dress up for the winter ball or play a musical instrument I was unable to be present for. I revel in those moments.

Zuckerberg is a household word. I wonder if he knew his invention; Facebook would become a household word as well.

I KNOW, I SAW IT ON FACEBOOK

When I told a friend I had lunch with that I've been cooking all day for a family gathering and her response was, "I know… I saw it on Facebook." I begin to wonder if I spend too much time posting the doings in my life. Most of it trivia, not always details and yet I don't ask for forgiveness for being a part of a discriminatory community, one that is there for company on a lonely day; one that you feel an integral part of where ever you go where you can make a choice to connect or not connect but rather in effect scan to places far and wide across the globe through links posted. Facebook is not only a place, it is a world apart and yet a "part" of society. It is a permanent movement across the globe.

Some do know that *"the world is full of trickery"* as Facebook becomes more and more like the world. However, it is a world you can control! At the same time it is a world unto itself. Where you can free fall emotions and later delete them when your mood improves and some of your revelations embarrass you and may even surprise you. But it's out there in the universe the minute you hit the 'post' key... Your grief, love, your inner thoughts, and creative ideas all reach the Universal mind and the replies you receive can take you down a path you have not considered. There is so much to be learned and Facebook has become the classroom of this century where you are allowed a voice back to the professor, an opinion and a mirror to your own inner lecturer.

PET LOVERS

Not a day goes by on Facebook when we don't see pictures and videos of dogs and cats. So many members are proud to show the world the wonders of their pets. Smiling dogs and talking cats appear on our feed making us grin or smirk, and often making us laugh out loud. At any length… we emote.

I've seen cats run across keyboard and jumping up on a counter to grab and eat food humans have prepared for themselves. One day I watched a cat knock down a Christmas tree while jumping up on a dangling decoration. Dogs talk on Facebook and I believe if they could type they'd post reprimands to their owners. Their humans design videos of themselves having full conversations with a pet. Pet lovers are like parents who adore their children. What I found extremely touching is the way Facebook causes so many pets to be rescued, adopted and saved from a dreadful fate in a kill shelter.

I'm guilty of loving my little Coton de tulear girl, Juliet! I chat with other Coton owners in a private Facebook group and we exchange some fun stories about our little friends.

PRIVATE MESSAGES

PM's have taken me out to lunch

I've said these words many times: "If not for Facebook" and I'll say them again. If not for Facebook's private messages, I'd probably not know the true pleasures of lunch dates, art classes, lecture seminars; motivational speeches that helped me rethink certain issues I've dealt with. Perhaps I'd never had experienced lunch in the Providence Art Club, a historic place where local artist's share their work for the public to see, admire and buy. Nor would I have sat in the Founder's room with the beautiful fireplace and books to enjoy a friendship and conversations about life, love and children with a great artist.

I would not have had so many Facebook friends invest their trust and caring into my life.

Without a doubt the egos are having a great time sharing pieces of their lives on Facebook. I love to share my paintings and my published books with other artists whom I admire. As for writing books, I do not believe I am the smartest person in the room. I write about what fascinates me and Facebook definitely does that. And when that happens, I become a *'talking machine.'*

LINKS, TO KNOWLEDGE

Facebook can lead the way to help better your lives by way of links. Some make Dr. Phil and even Sigmund Freud look badly lit.

Something I had never shared on Facebook had been causing me despair and interfering with my life.

I've never experienced anxiety before and thought it might be something that didn't truly exist. When others talked about it I thought my good advice would cure them.

For a few years I've been having a problem when driving on the thruway. It only happens then. My throat closes and my heart races and I feel like I will lose control of my car when I drive faster than 30 miles an hour. I've fought this, not knowing why it was happening to me. I've been driving since age 16 and have driven all over the country. I enjoyed driving. Now I can't feel safe whether I'm driving or as a passenger and it has gotten progressively worse this past year. This problem has a huge effect of my comings and goings. I have no problem driving when I'm not on the thruway and must take the long way where ever I go.

Though Rhode Island is small it takes me one hour to go 30 miles to my daughter's house by way of side streets from Providence to Coventry. If I drove on the thruway it would take me 25 minutes. This is upsetting and though I researched "Driving Anxiety" and tried to use the helpful hints, it didn't help me. The last time I drove on Rt. 95 it was 4:00 AM and I was coming home from the airport. There were no cars but mine on the thruway. When I accidently drove up the entrance I felt fear rip through me. I shook from head to feet and couldn't drive faster than 15 to 20 miles an hour until I found the first exit. I pulled over and breathed deeply for a while, then continued my journey home via side roads while praying out loud until I arrived safely. I didn't understand why I believed I was in danger alone on the thruway when there was absolutely no danger. I prayed almost every day and often got on my knees begging God to take this problem from me. I was becoming obsessed with it.

One of my sleepless nights caused me to turn on my laptop and go directly to Facebook where I found a link that led me to another link which led me to a site advertising help for anxiety attacks. In it there was a list of professionals who specialize in curing anxiety and podcasts of interviews with those professionals and the criteria that allows them to treat this dreadful disorder that made no sense to me even though it was real and causing me to become afraid to drive. I almost didn't open the link because I researched it so much I had given up without answers.

I watched the first podcast interview of a physiatrist who had at one time suffered (*of all things*) driving anxiety and he went on to describe the exact symptoms I was experiencing. I thought God was in the room.

After listening to the expert speak for a while and hearing him say the fear is real but the danger isn't something in me calmed down. He went on to say there is a way to end the attacks by way of getting to the bottom of the cause. He adamantly refused to blame the anxiety on genetics. He mentioned that it may be learned behavior. I get that. My mother was a nervous wreck most of my life and suffered from panic at times which my siblings and I witnessed as children, but my doubts remained because I never felt this while driving before my fifties.

"What underlying cause?" I wondered, could possibly cause such a problem in my life? For a long time I felt every emotion including anger about this problem. Little did I know Facebook could lead me to the solution without me having to share my feelings on social media. My hope is that someone suffering this malady will get help from the podcast I saw in the wee hours of the morning the way I did.

I saw Earnest Hemmingway's home on Facebook

CONNECT

I cannot say I've become more intelligent but my knowledge has widened to a broader range because of Facebook.

Meeting a stranger because of Facebook is now more common than being in their lives any other way. We have a firsthand opportunity to know them on a deeper level as we read their thoughts, enjoy their sharing and identify with their emotions in every stage.

"I HATE FACEBOOK!"

I've heard this a few times from people who decided to resent Facebook because they read things that cause them to feel intruded upon. While posters send information that seems trivial or stupid to some, I noticed the haters continue to examine the information day after day and shout out to those posters who bore them or seem to give a personal insult to their beliefs. A friend who "Hates" Facebook once said, "What's with that jerk who posted about Trump being a good president?" I just smiled. Another "former" friend told me she would unfriend me if I said anything good about Donald Trump. I unfriended her instantly. I have no like or dislike for Donald Trump.

What I once thought was a good friend sent me a private message to say, "How dare you insult Hilary Clinton! Don't do it again!"

I didn't consider what I said was an insult. I just referred to her as a political career criminal and added an LOL! I did *laugh out loud* a second after I read her Private Message.

Another friend debates continuously while hating Facebook. My point; everyone wants to be heard and what better place to do that? I learned quickly not to reply to political posts.

The beauty however rings out every day *on* Facebook. The love, compassion and sincerity are glowing constantly. Certainly the lovers outnumber the haters. When I read beautiful interpretations of life while enjoying my morning coffee it can be the platform on which I begin my day.

Reminders from the Facebook community that life is beautiful is always relating to the basic beauty of human beings. When a person asks for prayers and gets them I've seen prayers do their job on Facebook.

When I see horror in the shared news that upsets me, I pray immediately. Sadness doesn't go unnoticed and stories about pain and suffering reach our weak knees yet inspire us to be beholden for the good in our lives. Passing hope forward is almost a responsibility inherited from hope itself.

Before Facebook arrived in our lives, I doubt we ever thought too deeply about the words trust, depression, energy, illnesses, menacing foods, travel, betrayal, love, honesty and on and on…

Knowledge is key when we read weighty studies on any given subject daily. The examination of life and death can run into the end fact that we all will one day breathe our last breath and we all need to remember to be kind to each other and not take life for granted.

I personally enjoy the videos of motivating speakers who take us into their hearts with fantastic reminders to reach higher, not apologize for the lows and remember to touch life with our hearts instead of our minds.

Take Facebook out of our lives and we may be left with only the information we've mentally gathered in life to repeatedly scratch against. Without new entries of information that stream into my mind I doubt I could rely only on what I've learned before Facebook was invented. I'm now acutely aware that there is more to know.

UNSPOKEN LOVE

One of the many features of Facebook that I sense deeply is the way love can be spoken without leaving a letter that tells of love from beyond the grave. Unrequited love has no place on Facebook. It is usually returned.

Every day mothers, sisters, brothers, and Facebook friends speak to love on every stage. Out loud, "up front and personal" and with sincerity. How beautiful I find the expressions in videos and personal mentions of the joy and gratitude in life, and honor to someone we are not able to visit in person every day.

Love is not only a four letter word. It is an infinite emotion that can be applied to each other from toes to head and from art to the application of appreciation for nature. What other purpose could love be used? Love and suffering have visited all of us from the day we were born. Letting go of the suffering is the true way to complete love and

Facebook has led me there by way of expressions from those who have found the way out of pain. I confess, the path was subtle at first yet it continued on a silent level as I read and absorbed the messages I could not have understood any other way. Thank you Facebook friends, for the song.

FACEBOOK IN THE WORKPLACE

A job interview can go wrong in seconds regardless of your credentials which may fit the criteria for the position you were educated to fill.

Almost every corporate person with the power to promote your future position on the latter will find you on Facebook and examine your behavior before making a decision to hire you or not.

Your birthday celebrations where you appear drunk in pictures or use profane language along with your past jobs and reasons for being fired will show up and allow the interviewer to make a judgment on your capacity to represent their company. Videos are worse; especially live videos of your rants on life and dropping the F bomb in the fog of cannabis steam could permanently end your employment because Facebook posts remain indefinitely. More than this, Facebook can do financial harm in your business affairs. This happens on Facebook constantly.

College applications entered by brilliant students who play *on* Facebook are causing colleges to refuse applications and expel students who party and post.

Lives are affected in appalling ways on Facebook, as well as in good ways. There is a proper way to use Facebook. There is such a thing as Facebook protocol.

Some members of Facebook are 100% naked.

GIVE US THIS DAY OUR DAILY BREAD

My heritage is Italian. Cooking is part of who I am. I love to feed people. I chose to go a bit easier on myself physically after many years of very hard work in restaurants I opened. But I missed being in the business. Restaurant work is tough. I've compared it to torture some days. With burns on hands and cuts on fingers while swollen feet beg for a reprieve, I still love it. This is why when I am in a "first-class" restaurant I bow my head in appreciation to the owners and the workers. However, I am also a huge restaurant critic. I know how it works, and when I see laziness or bad food I do not forgive. My loyalty to "Owner operated" restaurants is always on.

Because I engage in Facebook I have traveled all over the world to see the foods conducive to the natives in each country. And have found recipes I imitated that ended up on my table. Some I could not imitate but remembered them as works of fine art.

I boiled some brussel sprouts, smashed them flat with a hand held potato masher. I then put them in a casserole dish and sprinkled olive oil, parmesan cheese, and mozzarella on top and baked them for 15 minutes. When I served them to my husband he liked them and asked how I did it. I told him and he knew immediately, "*I saw it on Facebook.*"

BAD NEWS-FAKE NEWS-REAL NEWS

Among innocence, naivety and other needs that validate your own anger and feelings of hopelessness , many in your face terror filled news articles, photos and videos of things that happen in other countries makes the media unable to write "Fake News" but the news people find a way. What was not "Fake News" happened on the days I saw OJ Simpson be found Not Guilty after evidence clearly supported his guilt. I saw a young mother who was arrested for killing her baby found not guilty also after seeing all the confirmation against her bleed heavily into our Facebook screen that spoke to her guilt. Those two events were not "Fake News"

Some may think the media is making them smarter. It's constantly bombarding and distracting them from thinking. They're unable to reflect on what they're hearing and reading and end up believing anything they're told.

This is compounded when news stories are emotionally charged. I guess this is the part of our brain that makes us most human. It's a neat trick and the very part of our brain the media speaks to.

I was reading Facebook posts earlier thinking to send my niece Rose a PM inviting her to celebrate Joe's birthday and got caught up in the news posts about the mass shooting in Florida. I stopped indulging myself in news programs on TV and later on Facebook because the thoughts haunted me for days each time I allowed myself to analyze the result of terrible information I couldn't change and yet I couldn't look away from.

Being one who won't allow myself to be taken into mob mentality my heart still felt feelings I would never have but for media. And I know media is business and business is media. The ads accompanying news related articles tell me so.

I might be well known as one who consistently reminds others that the world has not gotten worse. It was always messy. Media however has made the world more aware of the lowest parts of humanity and people gravitate toward those parts. Why? Perhaps there is a need to evaluate the good in us by comparison. I'm not sure but I do know bad news sells. But now days the problem is trust. What is not real is popularly being referred to as Fake News. That disturbs me. Real news is often bad enough and as we have been taxed out of our financial comfort by elected politicians, I hate when my intelligence is taxed. For this reason on most days I scroll past the painful headlines on the news posts.

I don't want negative thoughts in any dressing to play videos of blood and guts on my laptop screen. I'd much rather watch a child play with a Puppy, a story of survival, beautiful art, or listen to Don

McLean's Starry Night, a song I thought I'd forgotten. Those things keep my heart in check.

WORDS WEBSTER DOESN'T KNOW

It appears that Facebook has started a new language. Many acronyms lose me in their translation. A good friend had to teach his elderly mother that LOL doesn't mean, "Love a Lot." SMH means "Shaking my head." Excuse this but, STFU means "Shut the fuck up." LMAO means, "Laughing my ass off." ROTFLMYAO means, "Rolling on the floor laughing my ass off." doesn't unnerve me anymore. People usually respond with a smiling face. ☺

Smiles and tears are posted constantly by those too busy to write a response and they are genuinely sincere leaving no one to wonder how a post made them feel. How witty of the Zuckerberg team. Where else would we see these acronyms and little pieces of feelings?

MY POSTS

In the twilight of evening I write, paint, and look at pictures of my grandchildren. I read posts written by strangers on Facebook. I usually share windows of my life past and current. To be clear, not all of those windows revealed delightful times. Life changes like the phases of the moon. I want all of it and I want it sealed with a kiss.

I have an odd sense of humor and often post conversations between my husband and I that bring laughter. It's easy to get Facebook friends to my hidden table while we share endless cups of coffee and harmless laughter. My friends know my husband whom I often refer to as "Poppa Joe" even though he is not *on* Facebook. It tickles me to share his comical stories.

EVERYTHING IS ART

Am I an artist? It took me 20 years to say, yes I am. When paintings are finished I leave the art studio thinking, no one will like what I've painted. When I get the nerve to post one of my paintings I am always surprised to see the nice comments about it.

I've been convinced a few times to show my work at art fairs. When none of my paintings sold, I stopped painting for months. The reason I know I'm an artist is, I continued to paint at some point after the disappointment.

My best work comes to the canvas as a labor of love. It is hard for me to take money for my paintings but the ones I give away are appreciated and the ones people ask me to paint give me much pleasure. Paintings I've donated to many causes also make me happy. I just hope at least one day I'll be posthumous. I dare not look into my own eyes.

If not for Facebook I wouldn't know of all the treasures in history that sell for millions of dollars by artists, posthumous or not. Monet, Vincent, Renoir, Picasso and more artists' works are available for reflection on Facebook. I thank the contributors for educating me on things that are not trivial though inconsequential sayings and thoughts are also a form of education, especially art in all forms.

My love for art can inspire a reply from me when I see the wonderful works of artists I know and don't know. I might stare at a posted painting from a Facebook friend I've never met in person. I study the lines, color, light and shadows and think about how it came to be. Those are the works I love to share with others who find them as beautiful as I do. People like Anthony Tomaselli, an established Rhode Island artist that spares us no questions when his paintings come alive with New England scenes, New York City streets busy with that NYC energy, and with his Umbrella Series that I favor so. My constant question when I open Facebook and see his paintings is always, "How did he do that?"

Another artist I met on Facebook and one of my favorite artists is, David Short. I have never met him in person but I know him to his core because of his paintings. His expressions range from pure nature, to the magnificent images of women who share one commonality (elegance) by way of brush filled with color that seems to hold the image long before it appears on canvas. Something about his paintings makes me feel good knowing there is actually a way out of the likelihood that the life of an artist is one long, tender day. I could not have seen his work without Facebook.

My great photographer Facebook and virtual life friend is, Elaine Siwicki. Her flower pictures are out of this world beautiful and I always enjoy them.

In order to show all the art I've seen and favored on Facebook, I'd need thousands of pages, but I cannot withhold mentions from this book.

Another one of the great and much loved paintings is a portrait of her child painted by Barbara Ivy Green, whom I consider a "great" fine artist. Her portraits live and breathe as we enjoy the real impressions of the love she has for her child…

I cannot exclude Donato Beauchaine as another of my favorite artists who lives in Rhode Island. I am always fascinated with his clouds. I cannot imitate his work; I've tried.

I met a great artist from Manchester England. He taught me a few art tricks I won't forget and they helped me with many of my horizon paintings. His name is Stan Brookfield and he was kind enough to post videos of himself (via Facebook) painting skies that helped me paint them properly. He took me to England! His work is amazing and wins awards. His definition of an eagle appears on Facebook and no one can help but click the like and love keys.

I now consider Stan my "Friend" and have often thought about going to England to actually meet him. It would please me greatly to sit in one of his painting classes. He's one I consider a brilliant artist. I look forward to seeing his work posted *on* Facebook!

As I prefer good things to learn and find them on Facebook every day, I find it difficult if not impossible to cover them all in a book I have the nerve to write.

I think about what my father would say after he heard the answer to his question, "What the hell is Facebook?"

I may answer, "Facebook is an effective broad community of humans sharing thoughts, talents ideas and love in every possible form with billions of people all over the world."

I don't think it would be a good answer to a narrow minded intellectual. He might scoff me off as a diehard romantic and he would be correct.

 I see Facebook as a place not a thing. Perhaps it is like a room with voices coming in and out like room looks like when lights go on and off. Some of those lights shine upon areas of contemplation I'd never have researched. I wouldn't have without help from a forum filled with humans with something to say.

Reactions remain constant in the forum. Words beget words and some, like ammunition attack the innocence of the bewildered ones. I am often one of those people. Some of the words make me laugh till I cry. I like those best.

MAY I BORROW A CUP OF SUGAR?

Facebook is putting businesses out of business. Bigger than Craig's List, EBay, food chains, hardware stores, and many dry goods stores. Without leaving our chairs we can borrow a wheel barrel.

Selling your wares has become more profitable by way of Facebook than in any other method available today.

 Restaurants advertize using tantalizing pictures and videos to entice the diners out of their homes to enjoy what they saw *on* Facebook. You can even sell your home using Facebook!

Interest in dieting or baking scrumptious food is growing constantly while we scramble for the save link so we can go back and re read it later.

Ads are almost an irritant when they pop up on our screens when we're reading a story or watching a newscast about the death of one of our favorite actors or some educational review about anything at all... In the process that wipes out the story we're reading we search patiently for the X that will remove the ad and we continue reading till the next one comes along.

FACEBOOK FATIGUE

Some often complain that Facebook is not giving them what they want. Repetitious posts, ads, memes, and close up photos of someone's broken legged auntie, or an abused child can bring tears, and cause a mood change. Rarely do I say, "Enough!" But sometimes I need a Facebook break. I don't stay away too long because I know there is always a post that leads me to some outer limits of ordinary and I always learn something I didn't know. Information about every subject on earth and beyond gets me out of the package of restraint. When I see a post I do identify with, it validates me. I like to be validated. I'm also guilty of fishing for compliments.

Most of all I like it when a friend invites me to join a group or attend a celebration they don't want to go public with in a Private Message. Those are the things that bring me back after a few days away from Facebook.

SOCIAL MEDIA CHANGED THE WORLD

Suffice it to say, Social Media has brought people together in a colossal number of ways. I often wonder how it has met the needs we require to be informed or at least informed on more levels than before we had the internet in our pockets.

If I were to imagine social media as a family there would certainly be members I don't like, but my mind goes to the ways change for baby boomers doesn't affect the younger generation we call the Millennial's. I'd have to realize they don't know the world as we knew it. Social media is not all they know but it is absolutely a daily part of their lives. Baby boomers have one foot in each world. We are astounded by the scuttle of communication. The Millennial's are neither astounded nor fearful of allowing a slice of them exposed in their contact with the world, physically, mentally and emotionally. It works like a sort of freedom to them. (*A freedom they take for granted*) A teenager today can speak face to face via the internet, with their grandma in a different state. It's ordinary to them. I don't know exactly when I came to believe I'd seen everything and nothing was able to astonish me or get a reaction from me, and then it happened.

Until Facebook, lathered with pictures of abused children and animals, videos of riots, shootings, arts and entertainment began to prove me wrong I truly believed I had seen everything.

This morning I watched a little girl sing, Amazing Grace with a farmland background and a front porch. I got goose bumps while my hands were hugging my first morning coffee. She came through my lap top screen and into my kitchen then into my heart. She fascinated me with her beautiful voice. Before I saw her sing I knew, the voice is the most beautiful instrument in the world… She simply proved it once again and brought pleasure to my morning.

I've lost count of the singers, musicians and symphonies that have moved me that I could not have known *if not for Facebook*. Celebrated, comical entertainers have often brought genuine laughter to my life.

Some posts have brought sniffles and sparked deep thought while often inspiring me to pray.

UNFRIENDING- BLOCKING

As all Facebook members know, there are sometimes words not good to gulp down that have an effect on us in ways we would rather not see or want in our minds. Negative ideas or principles may infect our peace with sorrow and yes, anger. For those who need to exaggerate the truth are always sources of annoyance. Their words can plant a seed which will become a part of the creation of a mob mentality. Once the mob is active, separations of people begin to walk toward a weak point.

I'm aware of the struggle between good and evil. It is a war of its own merit. Nobody wins.

I step out of the circle and observe the veterans of the baby boomer life, I can detect the anger in strange forms and I can detect the frustration of those Godly souls who push love into every negative equation. While the optimist and the pessimist often shake hands but do not agree to disagree, I see human nature on every step. There will always be those who are not flexible and they worry me because there is no voice of reason that can get them out of the box where they feel protected.

The very words, "Outside the box" always made me feel safe. I can't imagine a life without change. And I cannot imagine staying still in my thinking.

Curiosity might cost me sometimes but if I didn't look over the horizon I could not know what I know today despite the price.

I reckon Facebook is well described as an enthralling odyssey.

If I didn't embrace change, I'd be dreary and alone. And if I didn't think outside the container I occupied before technology my inner self would be colored with dull paints.

I love the story of the two old men in the park sitting on a bench. One was smiling, throwing peanuts to the pigeons, chatting with passersby, and one was quiet and looked a bit tired staring into the park, seeing nothing.

The charismatic man had a life of change, many relationships with women. He suffered the pain of rejection and abandonment. The other man lived in a cold marriage for fear of losing his paid off home that they lived in for 50 years. He worked in one place till he retired and his marriage became a business arrangement... His friends were like him and most were dead. In his last years he sat in the park alone every day as a sad man who knew he couldn't change his past. Time for change is in the whirlpool of young years when so many make the choice to walk or fly through life. It isn't a matter of being safe or unsafe. It is a matter of living life in the mammoth classroom we've come to learn in. If we don't learn I have a strong feeling we'll have to come back to the same life all over again with knowledge and wisdom. What we discover here in life is ours for the taking.

I'm not sure how to say this about Facebook.

I don't always like what I see, though it's rare that my morning isn't enjoyed with some beautiful words, fine art, compassion and joy. It's rare because my friend's list is composed of loving people who don't punish me, themselves or life with negativity.

Because there are times when one or more of my good friends appears to be feeling down I have the opportunity to say something helpful... They enter heartache by different doors and that's okay. I want to embrace them and assure them that "tough days don't last but tough people do."

Some shoot passive aggressive written bullets and their negative posts are meant for one individual who may or may not know it.

It is noticeable that some Facebook members do not speak at all but rather click the "LIKE "feature and disappear. Some do speak about themselves, share pictures or market their wares but in no way reply to anyone's posts. Perhaps they are shy.

I enjoy Facebook for many reasons. It opens up a freeway of wonderful moments like never before. Sometimes it actually heals wounds in the hearts of those who have had to suffer through tragedies. In the wake of the death of a loved one so many people respond with kind words and good cyber hugs. It's beautiful to see that. I think the spirits appreciate those posts.

My passion for art is always satisfied when I see artists sharing their work with me. I get happy immediately when I see talent. Even puppies and kittens, and videos of babies are art to me. But mostly the faces of loved ones that shine so bright and the funny ways Facebook members approach life, I love best. I learned to appreciate laughter and I look for it every morning on Facebook when I need a pick me up.

Sadly this morning my coffee didn't go down well. When I opened my Facebook page the blaring news of *another* school shooting in Florida broke my heart. I saw dead children all over my news feed that did nothing to deserve to die but go to school in the morning.

There was no way to avoid that news. The effect of that incident will tear hundreds of lives apart. The new title that has come to be the "***School Shooter***" was caught and arrested.

I know a lot about Kansas and Missouri. I live in Rhode Island! My Facebook friends who live in those places took me there.

I learned how to paint shadows there too. I learned how to cook fudge (just last night.) I learned about the cats and dogs that need homes. I learned about coconut oil and how it keeps faces looking younger for $6.00. I found and reconnected with friends I hadn't seen in years. I've learned of, bought and read over 30 books I would have never seen if not for Facebook...

I learned that we are all the same, some more brilliant than others. They share that brilliance and I value that. I met many and came to love people all over the world! I see LOVE on Facebook every day and that is the best of all.

All I can really say is … Thank You, so I say it.

With this phenomenon called Facebook that has swept the new age way of communicating, we can reach out to the entire world. We can visit people in their living rooms miles away. We can be with loved ones in other countries when words are all we have to hug them with.

We receive information in our pockets, on our desk tops, and within the confines of our art studios, cars, jobs, and kitchens. This means of transportation of spinning wheels filled with information can make alterations on our lives.

The true definition of humanity is one click away. True is the entire spectrum, the actual power of life itself speaking to us day to day in ways we would not otherwise know and changing us in ways we could not have predicted while opening windows of our lives that total strangers can climb into.

Sharing every aspect of life, sometimes unwelcomed aspects, Facebook lets us accept or deny according to our own needs, the accessibility of information, suffering, hope, God, prayer, sickness, laughter, beauty, children playing, reconnections, healing, animal doings, counsel and song. We have become reachable, in every way.

I am trying to find the words to describe what Facebook is, and how it affects our lives while most are aware that over two billion people use Facebook to communicate every day and it's growing.

ON THE OTHER HAND

I've spoken to people who indulge in Facebook and there is an undercurrent of concern by those with too much time on their hands and those who feel addicted to social media. Posting from their work desks, kitchens, and in their beds during the wee hours of the morning basking in the blue light, some can't seem to leave. Facebook is an aside to life. It is always interesting whether we use it for sheer entertainment or to peek into some real life soap operas. Sometimes problems arise for those who are '*addicted*' in the way life outside of the Facebook world does not get lived.

People tell me at first they enjoyed seeing what their friends are doing, and it appears *on* Facebook they have amazing lives. People share mostly their best moments and events they want people to know about. They don't often post pictures of themselves in a miserable state. Though, some do fish for help when they are down, asking strangers to care, to sooth, to reach out to them. Between the lines you see they are saying, "Love me."

Facebook friends usually do reach out and it gives the person who posted their moments of anguish a *feel good* minute they couldn't get anywhere else.

It disturbs me to see a parent post a picture of their toddler covered with feces because I know it will be in cyber space forever… and one day perhaps, that child will be an adult who will suffer shame for the action of a mother or father and their behavior on Facebook.

I know life is not a steady stream of cheerfulness. Occasionally the painful parts sneak out in a post and later as Facebook shares my memories (*A feature Facebook creators added recently.*) I see a post I wrote on a "black dog day" years before.

When I see pain in anyone else, my body gets weak, however strong I profess to be. I mean literally, my legs feel wobbly every time someone with a talent for expressing their pain in words appears on my phone or laptop screen...

Dead mothers, dead children, dead husbands, brothers, sisters, those on the last lap of their lives summon my aching heart. Without exception I type a kind gesture because I can identify with the hurt. "On the other hand" within seconds, I will see a five year old child who will sing the sweetest song and those children repair my heart instantly. The sharing feature goes off like an alarm and I will turn my laptop around so whoever is in the room can benefit from it with me.

CHURCH AT SAINT FACEBOOK

It's Sunday morning and I reach for my coffee, turn on my laptop and greet the day with notes about my Italian preparation of foods my mother cooked while I was growing up. Tradition lives on at my house as I prepare the tomato sauce while meatballs, eggplant and pasta lay waiting for platters that end up on my Sunday table. I get visitors on most Sundays. Family members stop in to get a taste of Italian bread dipped in gravy, or a meatball or two and sometimes a dish of macaroni with good conversation on the side.

On days when no one comes I share the entire Sunday process on Facebook and enjoy replies from my friends.

Like church, I preach the sermon with amusement. Keeping the Sunday morning ritual within the limits of wit and pictures of food, I enjoy my Sunday mornings on Facebook!

EYES AND HANDS

When I look at photos on Facebook I can see behind the eyes of people, especially artists. The eyes betray the smiles. Hands speak loudly in photos.

I've been analyzing photographs for many years. The first thing I look at in a group picture is hands and the second thing is eyes…

.

AS FOR WRITING

James Patterson a well known writer of these times said, "Write a story, don't just write sentences."

As it took many years of painting before I could call myself an artist, it took longer for me to call myself a writer. It is clear that all Facebook members are writers. Some posts are crafted so well, I'm not sure why they don't write best sellers.

With a fresh pot of coffee nearby and a keyboard, I find writing effortless. If you asked me to write ten pages on the subject of ants, I could write up an avalanche of words that talked to and about ants.

Since being published for the first time in junior high school, in a year end booklet where 9th graders were asked to contribute a poem or short essay I'll never forget, while walking to class I was stopped by the guidance counselor who complimented my poem. I was painfully shy and certainly had a lot to say but my face became red and hot and I skipped off to get away from the compliment. (But I never forgot it) I was 14 years old and from that day forward I wanted to be a writer.

The first book I wrote was about the painful marriage of a friend. I was 19. It was 1969 and the world around me was changing from the life I created for myself in stubborn ideals while my peers were running off to Woodstock, abandoning their bras and with sunflower paintings on their Volkswagen Beetles. As the Vietnam War was raging I lost touch with my generation. Masses of drugged up teens were creating the term, "Anti Establishment."

I became the mother of four children at age 26 and I was out of the loop of the baby boomer generation and didn't' know till now that my brain wasn't fully developed and wouldn't be till age 27.

With little form of entertainment but for black and white TV, used books I bought for a dollar began to fill my house. I wanted to talk with ink.

My first book seemed good to me until I showed it to my father who critiqued it so harshly I didn't write for a long time but I was bugged so I wrote poetry to my children and by no means showed it to anyone.

What I had to say became stories I would type on an old borrowed typewriter. At first I wrote in a passive way. I spoke to my children about who they were in a makeshift book I hand bound in a photo album. I'd call that my real first book and it was appreciated by my adult children who got to know themselves as children through me. I'll never forget the day my third child, Richie, who was a teen at the time called me at work in hysterical laughter, saying, "Oh my God Mom, this is hilarious!" That made me smile. I saw that book as a legacy to my four children. It also made me write more and read more. Those cheap used books I'd buy at an old bookstore in Strafford Connecticut were my main entertainment while I mothered four children and slopped hash in a diner at night in Bridgeport Connecticut, where we lived.

I struggled with words on paper until the home computer arrived which made writing easier. I no longer needed a dictionary or thesaurus by my side. A keyboard and screen became my friends along with a spell feature because my spelling needed help. I was ashamed of that until I read that Stephen King has a spelling problem too.

I refuse to write with fancy words or uncommon phrases. I feel most comfortable with ordinary words that don't force readers to skim over important messages within a story that would be better written with common words.

I thought about writers of the past who had no help from technology and read about their lives. A book I read called; The First Wife written by Elizabeth Hadley.

She told about her marriage to Earnest Hemmingway and mentioned how he wrote his books while standing up. It told of his fierce need for privacy when he was writing and how he rented a room apart from their apartment so he could hear the voices in his head and write them with his ancient typewriter. He wrote, **For Whom the Bell Tolls**, and at the end of his life, he made sure it tolled for him… on his terms.

The first book I wrote which became published was written while I was in pure anguish. It was not the book I dreamed of writing.

I began to journal while grieving the death of my 32 year old son. I poured the pain all over the journals. I showed it only with my keyboard on a laptop computer with no intention of sharing it with the public.

My husband read the journals and insisted I share them in a published book. It took him years to convince me to allow it to be published. **Why Whisper?** did not become a best seller but it brought me together with many members of Facebook who had survived the death of one of their children. We began to share ourselves with a world, dark and lonely, filled with others who suffer, and we embraced. That went on for a few years until one day I erased my website filled with memorials and notes to my son and myself. I didn't want to revisit that grief. I felt like I was ripping off a scab only to bleed the same blood I worked so hard to clean up. The truth is I didn't want any more people to know how my son died or why he died. I didn't know then that the truth is what people wanted.

My game face was always on high without drugs or alcohol. Those two things were the only things I feared. I was right to fear them, they killed my son.

James Patterson was correct; we must *"tell a story, not just write sentences."*

ONE DREARY MORNING

I opened my Facebook link one day to be greeted by Antoine de Saint-Exupéry.

His Little Prince and his fox reminded me that;

"It is only with the heart that one sees rightly."

BABIES

Within a few years after my son left this earth seven grandchildren came to make the good in life to bounce around my broken heart and healed it with their laughter and their innocence. I thought if they could be happy while their Nawny is broken, so could she be. I studied them and saw their brilliance and their ability to live in the moments they spent finding the glory in life. I knew they were not yet taught to be concerned about anything but themselves; what they wanted, and things that made them laugh. Popcorn made them happy. Colors delighted them and strange noises made them curious. Dora the Explorer and Sponge Bob held their attention. They were distracted from their other surroundings and they instantly began to laugh when they played in the kiddy pool. They enjoyed simple pleasures like my garden hose, and as they grew old enough to walk and talk my heart got filled with information I hadn't noticed children possess. When I posted the videos of my little people playing, hundreds of people noticed along with me.

I knew then that children are not instruments or toys that are born to make adults happy and I began to study them closely.

I watched them learn to walk and talk. I watched their happiness. Did you know a one year old can sit in a noisy airport and still giggle? In fact, unless they're hungry all they do is smile. I thought of the biblical passage that reminds us to *"Be like the children."* and that's when I began to understand that children don't yet know how to worry about lost causes. They don't imagine the future, and they do not care about the past. Children live totally in the moment and are distractible instantly when you show them a bright color, their own shoe, or a cookie. How wonderful to be a child! With no inhibitions they run to you with a drawing they made with pride all over them. They are proud and pleased with themselves when they accomplish anything new. Unlike adults who are ashamed to show the world who they really are. Children do not know what passive aggression means. They are direct, and between age three and four are accused of being narcissistic because they're not afraid to ask or demand what they want and they get it. They learn quickly about noise control.

WHAT POSTS DON'T SAY

Every post you read on Facebook is a little story. Each story speaks of the life of the author. It is not difficult to get to know each member by way of what they don't say. I believe artists are the main mysteries on Facebook. One would have to read their paintings to know them. I study those. I am sure the shyest people among us want you to know how they feel when they give us the dots and hope we will connect them and get the picture.

FACE FACEBOOK

It is here to stay though Instagram might compete to a small degree. I do not indulge in Instagram. It is said it's for kids who will grow up and graduate to Facebook.

Mark Zuckerberg designed Facebook from his Harvard University dormitory room on February 4, 2004. He was assisted by his college roommates and fellow Harvard friends. Mark launched it.

How could he or anyone know how far Facebook would go? How interesting that Mark Zuckerberg was in touch with what people needed… a connection!

SUICIDE ON FACEBOOK

Yes there are those lost souls who live in complete aloneness who have videoed themselves taking their own lives. They were saying goodbye to the bullies, the haters and the soul crashing words from people in more pain than they were, and who use words to degrade and project some shallow hatred to strangers. That can happen because Facebook is a place not a thing. Words hurt face to face, and words written on Facebook for the sole purpose of injuring minds and hearts alike is very effective and I've seen the impact. The force of someone's hate often puzzles me because I know how easy it is to delete anything negative immediately on a computer. It's better than real life in that way and to be sure, the attacks are made by people who never met the victim. I do not, will not and cannot watch such videos. But I understand how words can be more hazardous than bullets.

WHEN EGO NEEDS A POLISHING

I give a piece of myself to a worldwide community of human beings who are willing to share their thoughts, ideas, humor and emotions. Loneliness is no longer a creature haunting the corners of our lives. With the click of a button we unite and share parts of ourselves in every situation.

There are people who are house-bound for many reasons. Some are handicapped and are not free to socialize in public. Some are grieving and refuse to leave their homes for a spell yet find distraction and often soothing strokes from others who grieve via Facebook. Some are responsible for loved ones in poor health and are unable to leave them. They are the people who need Facebook the most and are given the pleasure of enjoying the entertainment found on Facebook, no matter the hour.

It was through others my life took to travel on a road of emotional schooling.

It wouldn't be possible to count the ways Facebook changes lives. Mainly it shows life in every possible pose. With a broad view of the Middle East I learned things never taught in school. Natives of foreign counties often show up face to face with us on videos that appear on a computer screen, and tell us their stories. It's nothing like reading a book. In the event we fail to get the true message, we can replay their words.

One night while I was feeling down I opened Facebook and a video of Joe Koy appeared in a post by a friend. He began his sketch on a stage and told a story about his Filipino mother who used Vicks Vapor Rub to cure everything... I laughed till tears ran down my face and pieces of Joe Koy began to fill my Facebook wall until it contained videos of every show he ever performed.

Laughter is definitely healing. I fell asleep with a smile on my face that night.

I still laugh when I think of Joe Koy…

THE WORLD PRAYED FOR DORIAN ON FACEBOOK

Millions of people are being touched by a little boy who showed it how to love.

Thank you Dorian, the whole world has its arms around you.

A little boy who was diagnosed with cancer repeatedly fought the good fight like a boss! His mother blogged his transition keeping the world posted in his prognosis and his care. We got to know Dorian *on* Facebook, his struggles, joys, pain and his strength.

He told his parents that his greatest wish was to be famous in China. I venture to say that at his young age he didn't realize the impact his journey would have.

From America to China and all of Europe, photos of foreigners holding up signs that read, #D STRONG along with celebrities and millions of people Dorian never met.

Dorian taught us two things; He taught us that God used him as an instrument to show the world how far reaching love is. And, he taught us that he did what he came here to do and used Facebook to help him do it. He taught us the power of Facebook.

WHAT IS REAL? WHAT TO BELIEVE

We have no way of knowing if a member of Facebook is posting something real. Many unload recklessly and I believe they are outnumbered by honest sincere posters. But wonder and intuition rears its heads continuously and we need to judge for us what is real and what is not.

There is evidence of growing compassion and the world in a nutshell is a surplus of personal insights inspired by words and feelings posted in black and white on Facebook by people who need to safely share their underbelly filled with emotions that desperately need to be released.

There are a few people I met on Facebook before meeting them in person and learned they were truly who they said they were *on* Facebook. They are now my true friends and I get to enjoy them any time I want to.

It is sometimes said, "Nothing on Facebook is real" And I beg to differ. Sure it's true (*most*) people often mention only the good things in their lives on social media. They show pictures of the better sides of their faces. This may cause some who are in the throes of grief, divorce, financial crisis, or in the darkest places emotionally and mentally to feel irritated. They're not jumping for joy reading posts from people with perfect lives. Perhaps part of them cannot see what isn't said. They can't see what is behind the front door of some of those beautiful homes. Most lives on Facebook are air brushed. And why is that important? It isn't. Yet, there is no doubt some Facebook circles appear like a shrink's lounge where sad people gather and tell their sad stories daily. As an arm chair psychiatrist I'm guilty of trying to fix some of those gloomy people. I've sent books, songs, paintings, happy promise and so much of my energy.

Facebook is no longer a far-fetched way to join the living beings we've come to call friends and become influenced by them.

Now for the other side of the coin; it doesn't matter who is real or who is sitting in an attention chair spouting their feelings and truths. We need to see ourselves through them.

Today *on* Facebook I watched a video of a beloved family member's pictures and songs after he left earth. As the photos slowly moved across the screen of my laptop saturated with moving, tender songs that spoke to his life, I felt privileged to be allowed to see within the memories of a world I lived and loved in. It was the most beautiful thing I've ever seen because it was truth on every level.

Instead of crying, my mind went to the reason his 39 years on this earth happened. His love changed us. His love saturated and was returned by those affected on Social Media and I wouldn't have missed that for the world. He maintains celebrity status, attracting hundreds of friends to join the real life friends who adored him… Godspeed Robbie Blue…. Thank you.

To make my point I speak to Robbie's life to show you most things on Facebook do happen in real life.

PIECES OF OURSELVES

Though there is more to life than social media and my observations can be classified as endless with regard to Facebook which I consider the mainstay of social media, I must end with saying; I do have a life off Facebook.

To be truthful, my family is my world, my life... We gather often with my children and their children. We communicate face to face and share our thoughts. We hug each other in real life. We smell each other's perfumes, we laugh together. I have friends I see as often as I can. We *do lunch* and we share our lives off Facebook. I drive to the market and don't take pictures of what I buy.

 I don't take pictures of people in long lines at the Mall. I get my hair done and mop my kitchen floor. I sit outside in my patio and have long summer talks with my neighbors and rake leaves in my yard, walk the dog, go to restaurants for dinner, listen to beautiful birds singing. I read good books;

spend time with my husband of 25 years who has enhanced my life.

I may share some of his humor on Facebook but our marriage is in our home. My life truly revolves around the rewards I worked so hard to make manifest. I retired at age 51 after opening, and operating five small, lunch restaurants. I've worked many jobs, from factory employment to cleaning houses. I didn't have glamorous jobs; I worked for my children so they could have glamorous jobs.

One of my proudest accomplishments is my motherhood. My second proudest accomplishment is breaking the cycle of dysfunctional life I grew up in. I'm not ashamed to say I did some serious work on myself. But I must give some credit to Facebook where I found many tools, some peace and some validation for my past collisions with life but mostly I found tons of wisdom that comes through the glass house that Facebook is.

Facebook links lead me to Universal Laws, church sermons, Godly song, glorious moments created by beautiful people, precious babies, elegant scenes, amazing art, history, psychological disclosure, shock, history and indeed the rabbit hole of incredible intelligence, not to mention stupidity and a great deal of laughter.

What I see on Facebook will never be enough to sustain me. I want more than beautiful pictures. I want to hold those newborn babies in my arms. I want to pet beautiful dogs and cats. I want to hold grief-stricken mothers and tell them to give their grief a voice so it won't defeat them. I want to be in the room to hear toddlers giggle. I want to tell a five year old a fairy-tale with my tenderness beside them. I do those things in my life without Facebook.

I've never heard anyone say, "What is Facebook? Even grandmothers appear on Facebook and people in the last lap of their lives. They showed me that learning never ends no matter our age.

FACEBOOK IS NOT A TREND

I believe Facebook is here to stay. It may replace email. And, it may be our most accepted link of all links to the world.

SPEECHES

I saw President Obama give a speech today *on* Facebook. And, I saw hundreds of replies. Most were not pleasing. We're allowed an opinion! We can delete that judgment if we find ourselves being bullied or verbally attacked by those who disagree with our political opinion and who find it fun to slap our faces with words.

The first-class, the beautiful, the dreadful, and the hideous go for a wild ride every single day on Facebook. Those rides are endless.

SUCH IS LIFE

I often wonder how much life I was able to witness before Facebook opened the portal to the world.

My heritage caused me to exist in a very small world. In fact I'd never met anyone who is not Italian or part Italian until I was 16 years old.

Facebook changed me in a multitude of ways simply by introducing me to places in Europe and the Mid East along with places I would not have seen in my own country because of links and generous posts on Facebook where I could see pictures and videos that made me feel daring enough to travel to those places.

Of course posts and pictures of my friend's garden in my own state made me smile as well.

I don't feel threatened by Facebook. Clearly most of my Facebook friends know me very well. They know what I love, and who I love. They all know who my favorite artists are and they know what I will respond to. They know I cook a lot and am an oil paint artist. They know I love to speak in parables. Needless to say, they know exactly what I look like.

Like most, I get in their faces with my face and with the faces of those I love. They know who I am because I allow them to. Some people in my life don't know me as well.

"Now is the time for all good men to come to the aid of their country…"

Millions of people are free to give thanks to the veterans who served our country… because of Facebook.

THE PERILS OF FACEBOOK

Millions of Facebook participants delight in the fact that people they haven't seen in many years are able to find them and reconnect with them. At the same time, many get upset when they see people they are not comfortable with are able to connect with them also. This issue has caused many to leave Facebook.

Marriages and other relationships have been affected by that feature as well, and Facebook is often used as a dating site. It is not unusual for singles and also married users to become smitten with profile pictures. More often than not profile pictures do not depict the actual person's current looks. Of course there are Photoshop incidents that recreate a current picture. I've heard stories of people who actually set up a date with someone they met on Facebook that didn't turn out well when one or the other showed up looking nothing like their profile picture.

Facebook is not exempt from pedophiles posing as young men or women who lure teens away from their homes.

Teens are sometimes seen posing on Facebook in provocative ways. They are posting *selfies* that tempt sexual responses and are unaware of the reason that it is dangerous. Of course they are beautiful but don't realize their beauty can cause them harm. This seems to have died down this past year.

The latest craze is the facial distortions young users enjoy posting. For the longest time I didn't understand why making their lips appear like duck lips was so popular until someone told me it was a sexual draw. I'm going to venture to say that behavior is inspired by their peers and they find it funny. Duck lips still perplex me.

Fewer young people use Facebook lately but those things I mentioned are now happening on Instagram. Facebook is now being populated by older people. I enjoy sitting at the round discussion table with my fellow baby boomers. I can identify with most of them. I cannot identify with millennialism.

Another factor that upsets Facebook users is getting friend requests from virus gurus from foreign countries. It's been known that many have had their personal information and identities stolen when they accept the friend requests from such people. When I was a Facebook rookie who accepted all friend requests, sometimes the result was the black screen of death greeting me when I tried to open my laptop. It cost me a few new computers. It also caused my credit card to be whacked.

I was taught by one of my Facebook friends how to block individuals who request friendship with me, and with whom I'd rather not engage… It is a safety aspect.

Often someone will post a lovely paragraph about life, love or perhaps a caring cancer survival story. That post will include a request to have you share it by copy pasting it to your own news feed. This is also damaging in some way and some of your friends may refuse to do it and ask you to refuse to do it.

I frequently feel my cautious optimism sour when I see posts that ask for help to share what appears to be a beautiful thought.

I use the private setting that lets me allow only my friends and family to see what I post, although it prevents the public from seeing my books and paintings which in turn prevents me from using Facebook as a marketing tool that I sometimes need. There is however a feature that allows anyone to change the recipients from private to public.

THINGS I NEVER THOUGHT ABOUT

Written post by a Police Officer

"I have pulled dead, mangled bodies from cars...

I have lied to people as they were dying.

I said you are going to be fine as I held their hand and watched the life fade out.

I have held dying babies, bought lunch for people who were mentally ill and haven't eaten in a while.

I have had people try to stab me and fought with men trying to shoot me.

Ben attacked by women who have had the shit kicked out of them by their husband as I was arresting him.

I have held towels on bullet wounds.

Done CPR when I knew it wouldn't help just to make family members feel better.

I have torn down doors, fought in drug houses. I chased fugitives though the woods.

I have been in high speed car chases.

Foot chases across an interstate during rush hour traffic.

I have been in crashes, been squeezing the trigger about to kill a man when they came to their senses, and stopped. I've waded through large angry crowds by myself. Drove like a mad man to help a fellow officer. Let little kids who don't have much sit in my patrol car and pretend they are a cop for their birthday.

I have taken a lot of people to jail, given many breaks. Prayed for people I don't even know. Yes and at times I have been "violent" when I had to be. I have been kind when I could...

I admit I have driven to some dark place and cried by myself when I was overwhelmed.

I have missed Christmas and other holidays more than I wanted too.

Every cop I know has done all these things and more for lousy pay, suckie hours and a short life expectancy. We don't want your pity; I don't care for your respect. Just let us do our jobs without killing us... Please."

Thank you

MY WRITER FRIENDS

It is common to see posts that reveal life on levels I had never examined. Words, thoughts and revelations abound and I feel insight widen when those things are exposed by users who have experienced events in their lives I've never known enough to contemplate, especially war veterans.

Writers have shown me war from a personal perspective and brought me to foxholes and blood baths in Vietnam. I cried from my deepest heart to learn what little truth we received about that war which took place in my lifetime. John Willis, the author of, **LIGHT CASUALTIES**, brought me with him and spoke to the hell he lived in and made it amazing that he survived and yet, his words gave you the feeling the war never ended for him. Though he carried that war within himself he was clearly one of the kindest veterans on Facebook. As painful as his story was to read, I could not stop reading. His pseudo name was JC

Willis and we became friends in real life. Not to say Facebook is not real life. We communicated for years. He sent me a handmade sculpture, and I sent him one of my paintings. Before long his wife Vickie became a beloved friend of mine as well. I so enjoyed her posts that showed her creations, cookies, handmade items that were so unique I commented on them so she would know how talented she is. They live in California and I live in Rhode Island but we felt like neighbors. I often promoted (shared) his book in order to hope young people might learn what they're not taught in school about that atrocious war and how the media lied to us. It should be required reading in every school in America. .

MEMORIES ON FACEBOOK

Every day people will post memories of anniversaries you may want to remember and repost. I do enjoy those of mine and of friends and family. It's fun to go back in time and see where you were and what your thoughts were many years ago. Facebook users have shared a past piece of their lives in various ways. Collections of their memories in hard copy books each year are available for a price and they're lovely. I received two of them from my daughter as gifts and these coffee table books have been enjoyed by people who have visited my home. Memories take on a new meaning on Facebook.

Memories and mentions of those we have lost often show sincere testimonies of their lives and tell how much they were loved. Facebook keeps them living.

Happy Birthday messages are sent to heaven by followers who respect and respond to them on their special days. This action pays reverence to the dearly departed. Facebook makes them remembered by thousands of people who never met them, but send love to them.

FROM MY BOOK,

NOTES TO MY CHILDREN

"What happens after death?

Life

There is no such thing as death"

RESCUED ANIMALS

While cooking dinner I left my laptop on while videos were streaming by. I heard a speaker tell about a huge turtle that became tangled in mesh while stationed on rocks on the shore of the ocean. I had to go look at the laptop screen. Angry waves were pushing and splashing until the turtle became stuck between two rocks. He continued to struggle until two men began a rescue. They saw one of its legs unable to move because along with the mesh there was a plastic bottle attached to it. They had no knife to cut the mesh so they began to use their fingers to unwind and pull it apart, which did little good. Waves got heavier, slamming hard into the men, and the turtle rescue seemed hopeless. When one of the men found a lighter in his pocket, he was able to burn the tangle and free the poor creature that swam away. I'm certain he was grateful.

Similar rescues appear almost daily on Facebook that involve all kinds of animals. I've seen videos taken by observers record how humans liberate dogs, cows, whales, deer, and so many incidents when human beings came to the rescue.

Where else but on Facebook would I see such things?

FACEBOOK HAS NO END

There is always more to say because minute to minute the enormous amount of people who speak using the mouthpiece called Facebook rises. It is never still. Information in massive amounts pours in continuously.

It would be impossible to illustrate the split second growth of formal and informal sharing of everything the world has to offer.

If my father was here and if I were to answer my father's question today; "What the hell is Facebook?" I would say, "It is a connection to the world. And now Nascenzio, seeing that you are *on* Facebook, maybe it's a connection to the other world.

It is enough to say, Facebook is the world and everything in it.

THE ENDLESS END …

Joanne Mazzotta

www.ingramcontent.com/pod-product-compliance
Lightning Source LLC
Chambersburg PA
CBHW052315220526
45472CB00001B/128